P9-CSE-662

The World of
CERAMICS
A Price Guide

by Pat & Larry Aikins

© 2000

Published by
L-W BOOK SALES
PO Box 69
Gas City, IN 46933

ISBN#: 0-89538-108-7

Copyright 2000 by Pat & Larry Aikins
L-W Book Sales

All rights reserved. No part of this work may be reproduced or
used in any forms or by any means - graphic, electronic, or
mechanical, including photocopying or storage and retrieval
systems - without written permission from the copyright holder.

Published by: L-W Book Sales
PO Box 69
Gas City, IN 46933

Please write L-W Books for our free catalog
of books on antiques and collectibles.

Table of Contents

Introduction to Ceramics

This book is filled with a variety of ceramics. Including Enesco, Ucagco, Kreiss, Wales, etc. Many were made in Japan.

In the 1950's, you could find ceramics in five and dime stores and souvenir shops for 19 to 99 cents. Today any of the older ceramics that you find are increasing in value due to rarity and demand of the ceramics.

Due to the low cost of production price, many of the ceramics were made in Japan. Most of the Aquarium pieces were made in Japan because of this reason. Then shipped to America.

The Enesco Company is still in business today. They have many, many series of ceramics they have produced. The Dear Gods and Human Beans are two of the series they made. The Human Beans are of course, shaped like beans. They have cute little sayings on them, such as "Be nice to me, I'm a Human Bean". The Dear Gods are ceramics with little girls and boys saying a little prayer.

There are a few pieces of the Kreiss ceramics that we added to this book that are out of, The World of Kreiss Ceramics, the book we just finished this year.

We very much hope you enjoy this book of ceramics.

Pat & Larry Aikins

Pricing

The values in this book should only be used as a price guide. They are not intended to set prices, which vary due to local demand, condition and availability. Auction and dealer prices also vary greatly.

Neither the author nor the publisher assumes responsibility for any losses that might be incurred as a result of consulting this guide.

The values on the ceramics are based on mint condition, no chips, fading or cracks in the piece and that the piece still have its original tag might it be the metal or the paper tag.

About the Authors

Pat and Larry Aikins are not strangers to the collecting fields. Pat has been a collector for the past 15 years of T.V. related toys of the 60s and 70s, character drinking glasses, typewriter tins, and Kreiss ceramics. Larry, who has been a collector since a small boy in Kansas, started with arrowheads, which he still enjoys collecting today. All through his life he has collected all types of things.

They have published 3 books, 2 on lunchbox collecting. The Pictorial Price Guide to Metal Lunchboxes and Thermoses and The Pictorial Price Guide on Vinyl and Plastic Lunchboxes and Thermoses. Pat and Larry have been collecting various ceramics for several years. In fact, they just had a book published on Kreiss ceramics, which is called The World of Kreiss Ceramics. Over the years they have expanded their collection of ceramics in which they show to you in this book.

Aquarium Houses

Orange Top House,
Japan, 2 1/4" h.
$18

House, Japan, 2 3/16" h.
$28

House, made in Japan, 2 5/8" h
$26

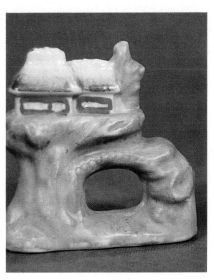

Blue Houses,
Japan, 3 1/4" h
$36

Blue House, Japan, 2 1/2" h
$26

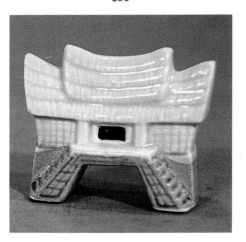

Pink Roof House, 2 1/2" h
$26

Aquarium Houses

Orange Top House, Japan, 3 1/2" h
$28

Japanese Areh, 2 1/2" h
$28

House, Japan, 4 3/4" h
$38

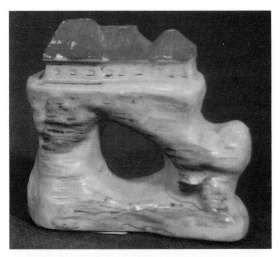

Orange Top Houses, Japan, 2 1/4"
$34

Little Town, Japan, 2 1/4" h
$38

Yellow Houses, Japan, 3 3/4" h
$28

Aquarium Houses

Japanese House, 2" h
$26

House, Japan, 3 1/2" h
$32

Aquarium House, Japan, 4 1/4" h
$36

Japanese Houses, 3 1/4" h
$28

Aquarium Houses

Japanese Houses, 4 1/2" h
$32

House, Japan, 3" h
$26

Blue House with trees, Japan, 3 1/4" h
$38

House with trees in columns, Japan, 4 3/8" h
$36

Aquarium Houses

Colored Japanese House, 4 1/4″ h
$36

Aquarium House, 6 3/10″ h
$34

Brown Korean House, 4″ h
$36

Japanese House by Hanaki, 1967, 4″ h
$38

Aquarium Houses

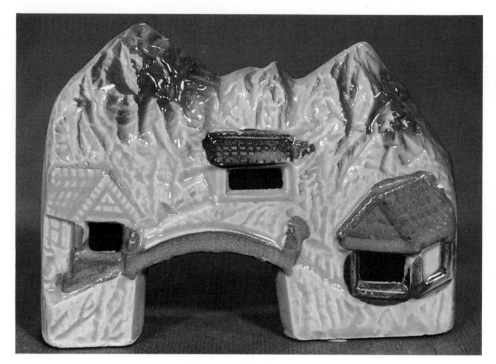

Mountain House, Japan,
3 3/4" h x 4 3/4" w
$32

Japanese House, 5 1/4" h
$46

Aquarium Houses

Pink Japanese Bridge, 4 1/2" h
$32

Japanese House, 6" h
$44

Japanese House, 4" h
$28

Blue Japanese House, 5"h
$40

Aquarium Villages

Village on a Hill, 3 1/4″ h
$38

Mini Village, 2 1/4″ h
$28

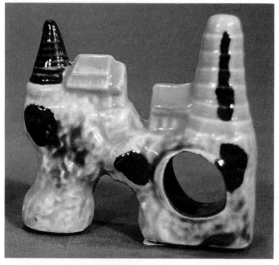

Village, 3 1/4″ h
$32

Mini Village, 2 1/2″ h
$28

Village, 3 1/4″ h
$26

Japanese Village, 4 3/8″ h
$36

Aquarium Villages

Cities on Hills, 4″ h
$44

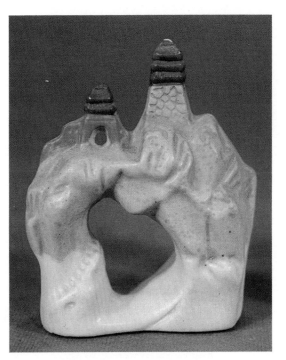

Hillside Houses, Japan, 3 3/4″ h
$34

Pink Village, Japan, 3 1/2″ h
$38

Aquarium Villages

Village, Japan, 3 3/4" h
$34

Village, 4 1/2" h
$36

Left: White Japanese Village, 4" h - $30
Right: Japanese Village, 4" h - $32

Aquarium Villages

Japanese Town, 4" h
$32

Left: Japanese House, marked "Made in Japan", 4" h - $32

Right: Japanese House on Hill, 4" h - $32

Aquarium Temples

Temple, made in Japan, 4" h
$30

Temple, Japan, 3 3/4" h - $34

Yellow Tower, 5" h
$24

Orange Tower, Japan, 3 1/2" h
$26

Speckeled House, 3" h - $12

Temple, 2" h
$12

Red Tower, 3 1/2" h - $28

Orange Japanese Tower, 3" h - $28

Aquarium Temples

Temple, 3 1/2" h - $29

Chinese Tower, 5 3/4" h
$32

House, 4" h - $32

Temple with columns, Japan, 4" h - $32

Blue Tower, Japan, 4" h
$28

Aquarium Temples

Left: Brown Temple, 3 3/4" h x 4 1/8" w - $26

Right: Blue Temple, 3 3/4" h x 4 1/8" w - $26

Left: Japanese House, 4 1/4" h - $28

Right: Temple, 3 1/4" h - $24

Aquarium Temples

Left: Brown Temple, 3 3/4" h - $26

Right: Pink Japanese Temple, 2 3/4" h - $18

Left: Japanese Tower, 4" h x 2 5/8" h - $28

Right: Blue Japanese Tower, 3" h x 2 1/4" h - $18

Aquarium Temples

Green Temple, 9 1/2" h - $32

Green Paragoda
7 3/4" h
$48

Blue-Green Japanese Temple
9 1/2" h
$32

Aquarium Temples

Maroon Pagoda, 4" h
$32

Brown Japanese Tower, 5" h
$16

Pagoda, 4 1/8" h
$32

Japanese Archway, 3" h
$26

Aquarium Temples

Orange Towers, 4" h
$28

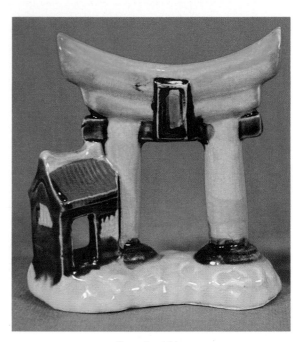

Temple, 4" h
$28

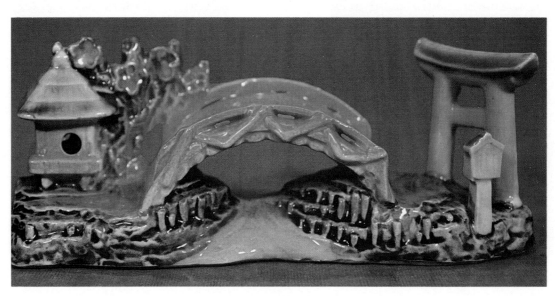

Japanese Bridge, 3 1/4" h
$44

Aquarium Towers

Japanese Towers, 5 3/4" h
$34

H Shape Japanese Towers, 2 1/4" h
$18

Tower & Bridge, Japan, 2 1/4" h
$28

Towers, 2 3/4" h
$24

Aquarium Towers

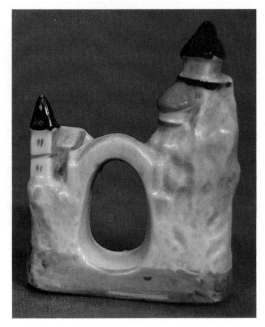

Black Top Towers, Japan, 4" h
$36

Blue Top Towers, Japan, 2 1/2" h
$26

Black Top Tower, 4 1/4" h
$36

Towers, Japan, 4" h
$28

Aquarium Towers

Orange House & Tower, Japan, 3 1/2" h
$34

Pink Top Towers, Japan, 3 1/2" h
$42

White Japanese Towers, 2 1/4" h
$18

Japanese Tower, 3 3/4" h - $34

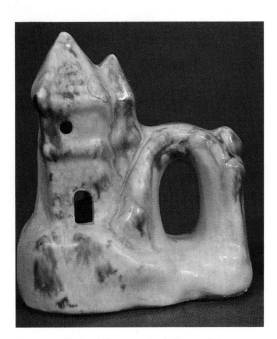

Washed Towers, 4 1/2" h - $34

Aquarium Towers

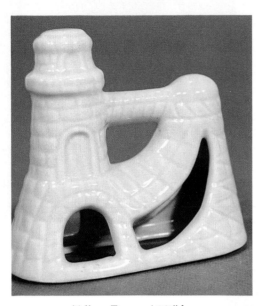

Yellow Tower, 4 3/4″ h
$36

Blue Towers, 4 1/2″ h
$34

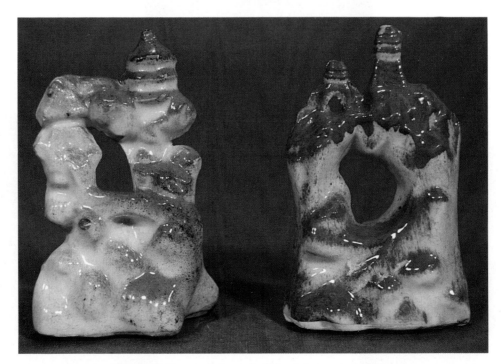

Blue Rock Towers, left one is 5″ h, right one is 4 1/2″ h
$24 each

Aquarium Castles

Castle, 3 3/8″ h
$34

Japan Castle, 3 1/2″ h
$44

White Towers Castle, 4 3/8″ h
$32

Castle, Japan, 4″h
$34

Colorful Japanese Castle, 3″ h
$28

Aquarium Castles

Green Castle, 5 3/8" h
$42

Castle Wall, Japan, 3 1/2" h
$20

Castle, Japan, by Hanaki, Zenith Product, 5" h
$46

Aquarium Castles

Pink Japanese Castle, 4 1/4" h
$36

Green Japanese Castle, 4" h
$36

Left: Japanese Building & Tower, 3 1/4" h - $30
Right: White Japanese Building, 2 3/4" h - $28

Aquarium Castles

Grey Castle, 6 3/5″ h
$44

Red Castle, 7 3/4″ h
$44

Aquarium Castles

Maroon Castle, 5 3/4" h
$44

Green Castle, 5 1/4" h
$48

Aquarium Huts

Japanese Hut, 5" h
$32

Japanese Hut, 4 3/4" h
$32

Brown Hut, 3 3/8" h
$28

Native Hut, 4 1/4" h
$34

Aquarium Huts

White Hut & Bridge, 2 1/2" h
$24

Hut, 6"h
$56

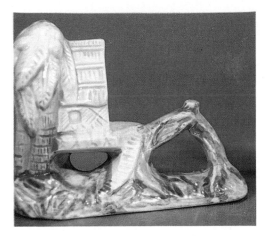

Blue Hut, Japan, 3 1/2" h
$36

Red Top Hut, Japan, 3 1/2" h
$28

Japanese Hut, 4 1/8" h
$48

Aquarium Huts

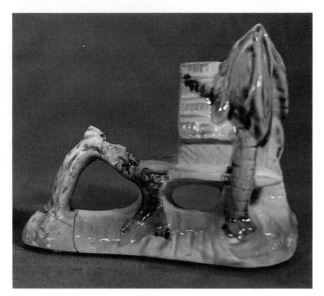

Hut, Japan, 3 3/4" h
$28

Japanese Huts, 2 1/8" h
$24

Japanese Huts, 4 1/2" h
$34

Aquarium Huts

Hut, 4 3/4" h
$38

Huts and Trees, 5 1/4" h
$44

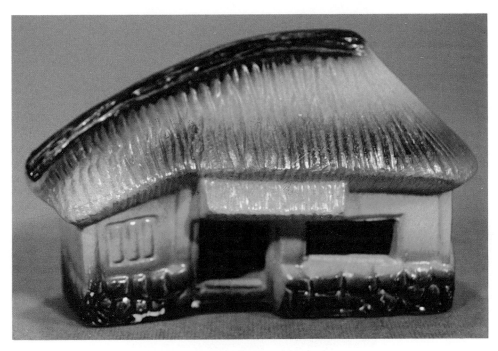

Yellow Hut, 3 1/4" h
$36

Aquarium Huts

Native Hut, 4 1/2" h
$34

Hut made in Japan, 6 3/5" h
$58

Native Hut, Made in Japan, 5 3/4" h
$38

Aquarium Lighthouses

Mini Lighthouse, Japan, 2 1/8″ h
$26

Lighthouse, Japan, 4 1/2″ h
$28

Orange Lighthouse, 4 1/8″ h
$28

Japanese Lighthouse, 6 1/4″ h
$48

Aquarium Lighthouses

Blue Lighthouse, 3 3/4" h
$26

Maroon Lighthouse, 4 1/2" h
$34

Black Top Lighthouse, 5 1/4" h
$38

Lighthouse, Japan, 4 3/4" h
$36

Aquarium Lighthouses

Green Japanese Towers, 2 1/2″ h
$22

Lighthouse, Taiwan, 3 3/8″ h
$36

Green Tower, Japan, 3 1/2″ h
$34

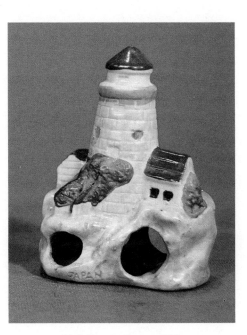

Lighthouse, Japan, 4″ h
$32

Aquarium Lighthouses

Lighthouse, Japan, 3 1/2" h
$32

Lighthouse, plastic, Penn Plax,
Hong Kong, 5 1/4" h
$36

Lighthouse, 5 9/16" h
$38

Plastic Lighthouse, 5 7/8" h
$22

Aquarium Lighthouses

Yellow Lighthouse, 4" h - $34

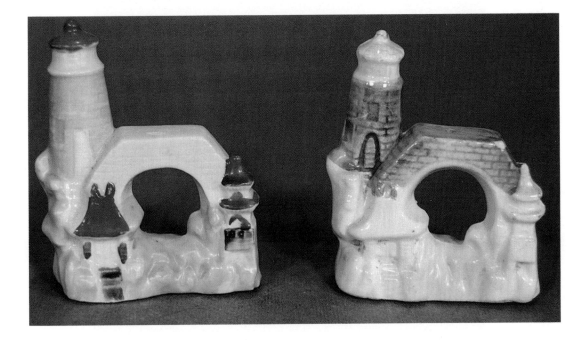

Left: Lighthouse, Japan, 3 1/2" h - $26

Right: Lighthouse by a bridge, 3 1/2" h - $26

Aquarium Lighthouses

Green Lighthouse, 3 9/16" h
$26

Left: Green Top Lighthouse, 5 3/4" h - $44
Right: Hand Painted Lighthouse, Japan, 6" h - $44

Aquarium Bridges

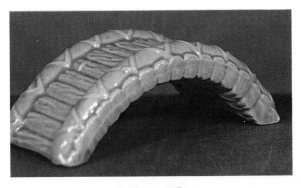

Bridge, 1/2"h
$20

Orange Bridge, Japan, 1 1/2" h
$20

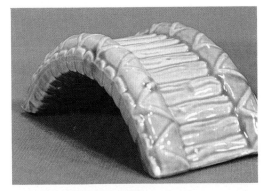

Brown Bridge, 2 1/4" h
$24

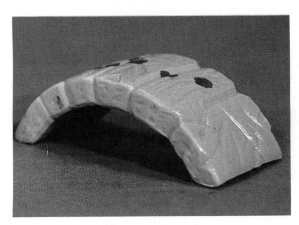

Green Bridge, Japan, 1 1/2" h
$18

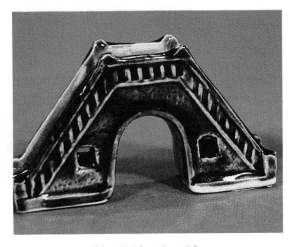

Blue Bridge, 2 1/4" h
$38

Aquarium Bridges

Green Japanese Bridge, 2 3/4" h
$24

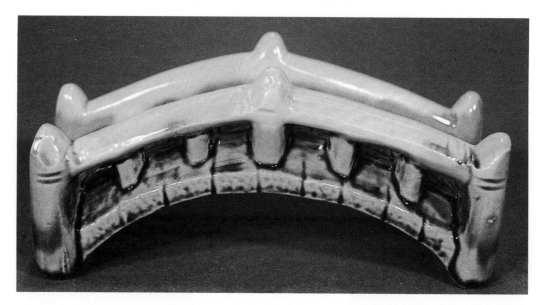

Bridge, 7 1/8" h
$22

Aquarium Windmills

Blue Windmill, 2 3/4" h
$32

Windmill and Houses, Japan, 3 3/4" h
$38

Aquarium Mermaids & Divers

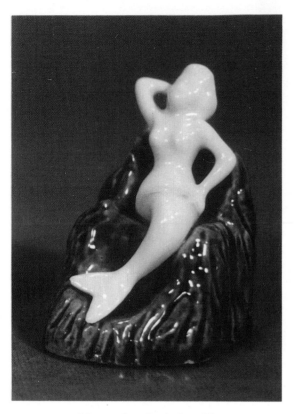

Mermaid on Rock, 2 3/4" h
$56

Mermaid in Shell, Japan, 2 1/2" h
$88

Laying Mermaid, 1 1/2" h
$62

Mermaid, 1 1/2" h
$84

Aquarium Mermaids & Divers

Mermaid, 2 1/2" h
$48

Mermaid, 4 1/2" h
$48

Mermaid, 4" h
$48

Aquarium Mermaids & Divers

Mermaid, 6 1/2"h,
SL Clutter 57, Hawthorne CAL
$89

Mermaid, 8" h
$89

Left: Mermaid, 2 3/4" h - $110
Right: Boy Riding Fish, 3" h - $120

Aquarium Mermaids & Divers

Mermaid, 4" h
$84

Mermaid, 5" l
$68

Mermaid, 3 5/8" h
$88

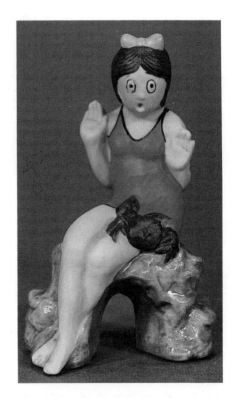

Sunbather, 5" h, marked with red ink
"Made in Japan"
$110

Aquarium Mermaids & Divers

Mermaid, 3 1/2" h
$88

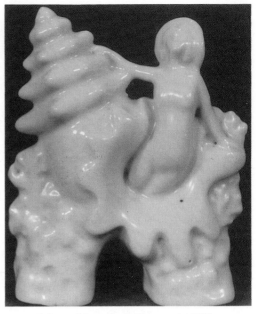

Mermaid on Rock, Japan, 4 1/2" h
$88

White Mermaid on Seashell, 5 1/4" h
$120

Diver & Mermaid, made by Zenith in
1968, 5 1/2" h - $70

Diver & Mermaid, Zenith, 1968, 5 1/2" h
$70

Aquarium Mermaids & Divers

Left: Mermaid, 3" h - $54
Right: Diver, 3 1/2" h - $110

Diver, Japan, 3" h
$65

Left: Diver, Japan, 3 1/2" h - $68
Right: Diver, Japan, 2 1/2" h - $56

Diver, Japan, 4 1/8" h
$56

Aquarium Mermaids & Divers

Diver & Octopus, 3" h
$74

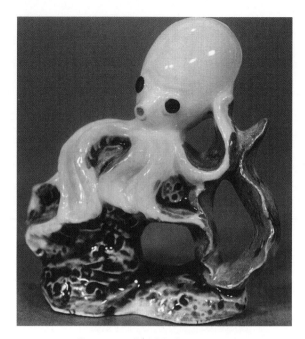

Octopus, 4" h, Made in Japan
$58

Diver & Octopus, 3 3/4" h
$74

Diver & Octopus, 3 1/2" h
$74

Aquarium Mermaids & Divers

Diver, 4 1/2" h
$72

Diver, 4 3/8" h
$68

Left: Diver, made in Japan, 5" h - $94
Right: Diver, 3 3/4" h - $65

Aquarium Mermaids & Divers

Diver & Chest, 5 3/8" h
$68

Scuba Diver
$55

Diver, Japan, 5 3/16" h
$58

Aquarium Fish, Whales & Frogs

Fish, Japan, 3 1/2" h
$28

Angel Fish, Japan, 4 1/8" h
$32

Large Brown Fish, 5 1/2" h
$38

Fish, made in Japan, 4" h
$32

Aquarium Fish, Whales & Frogs

Left: Fish, Japan, 2″ h - $20
Right: Fish, 2 1/8″ h - $22

Left: Fish, 2 1/2″ h - $22
Right: Fish, Japan, 2 1/8″ h - $22

Left: Fish, 1 3/4″ h - $20
Right: Fish, Japan, 2 1/2″ h - $22

Aquarium Fish, Whales & Frogs

Left: Fish, 2 3/4" h - $22   Right: Fish, 2 1/2" h - $22

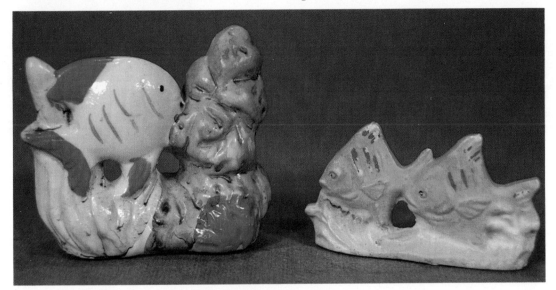

Left: Fish, 2 1/2" h - $22   Right: Fish, 1 1/2" h - $20

Left: Seahorse, 4 1/2" h - $45   Right: Seashell, 3 1/2" h - $36

Whale, bubble blower, 3" h - $42

Seal bubble blower, 3 1/8" h
$56

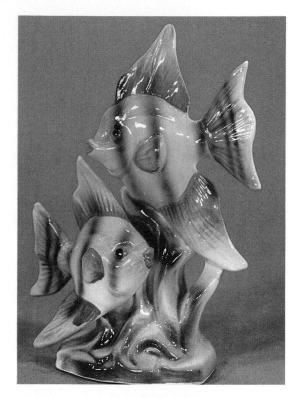

Angel Fish, 8" h
$56

Left: Frog, with engraved mark "Japan", 3" h - $26
Right: Coral, marked in black ink "Japan", 3 1/2" h - $26

Aquarium Fish, Whales & Frogs

Left: Goldfish, 3″ tall - $22
Right: Shark, 2 3/4″ tall - $24

Left: Pink Sword Fish, 3 5/16″ - $28
Right: Brown Fish, 2 3/4″ h - $24

Aquarium Fish, Whales & Frogs

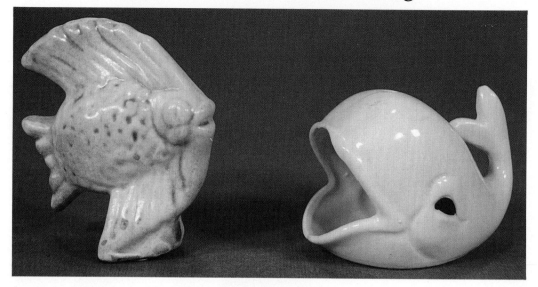

Left: White Fish, 3 1/4" h - $22
Right: White Whale, 2 1/2" h - $22

Left: Three Pink Fish, 3 1/8" h - $22
Right: Blue Fish, 3" h - $22

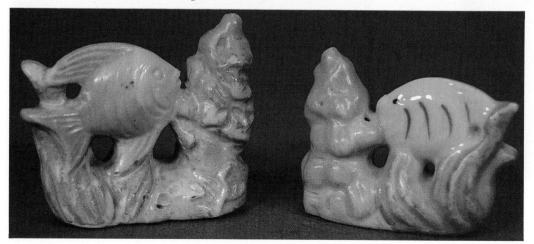

Left: Angel Fish, 2 1/2" h - $22
Right: Baby Blue Fish, 2" h - $22

Aquarium Fish, Whales & Frogs

Left: Orange Fish, 3 1/4" h - $28
Right: Blue Fish, 2 1/2" h - $22

Turtle, 2 1/2" h
$26

Turtles, 4" h
$34

Aquarium Signs

Kiss A Frog Today!! sign,
3 3/4" h
$22

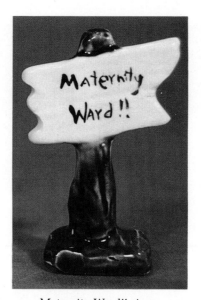

Maternity Ward!! sign,
4 3/4" h
$12

Sorry Charlie!! sign,
3 5/8" h
$24

Ye Ole Fishin Hole!!!
sign, 3 1/2" h
$18

No Fishing sign,
4 1/4" h
$24

Do Not Disturb sign,
4 1/2" h
$24

Aquarium Signs

Out To Lunch sign, 6 1/2" h
$28

Fishing Haven sign, 3 1/8" h
$24

Left: No Fishing sign, 4 1/8" h - $18
Right: No Swimming sign, 3 7/8" h - $16

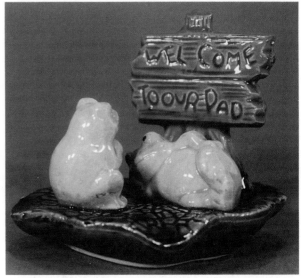

Welcome To Our Pad sign, 3 3/4" h
$24

Aquarium Signs

Do Not Pollute sign, 5 3/4" h
$28

Do Not Pollute sign, 4 1/2" h
$24

No Fishing sign, 4 1/4" h
$28

Aquarium Miscellaneous

Brown Rock, 3 1/4" w
$12

Rock, 3 3/4" h
$22

Sea Horse, 3 3/8" h
$56

Plastic Paddle Wheel Boat, 3 1/4" h
$36

Alligator bubble blower, Japan, 7" long
$85

Aquarium Miscellaneous

Hippo bubble blower, Japan, 2" h
$86

Hippo bubble blower, Japan, 2 1/2" h
$96

Left: Sail Boat, 3" h - $18
Right: Ship Wreck, 3 1/2" h - $18

Rock Formation, 4 1/5" h
$24

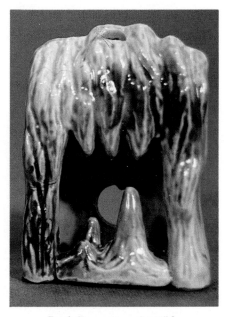

Rock Formation, 3 1/2" h
$22

Aquarium Miscellaneous

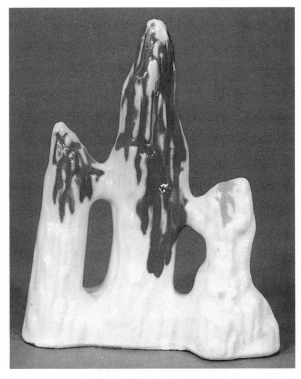

Lava Mountain, 5" h
$22

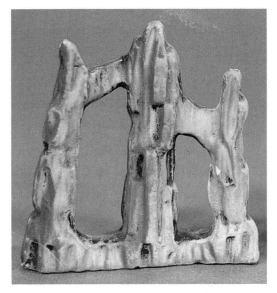

Rock Formation, Japan, 3" h
$20

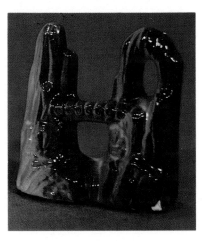

Rock Formations, 3" h
$20

Psydeum., 4 3/4" h
$34

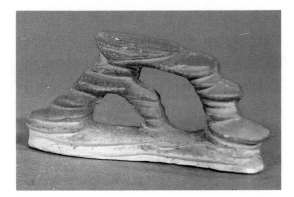

Miscellaneous, 2" h
$18

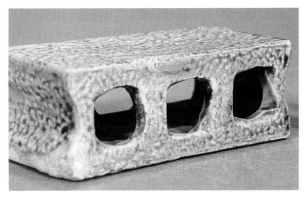

Brick, 2" h
$12

Aquarium Miscellaneous

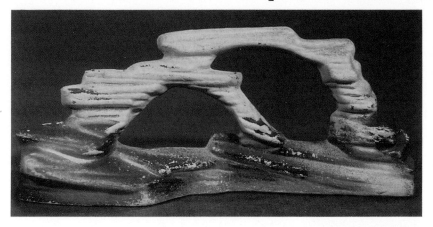

Rock Formation, 3" h - $14

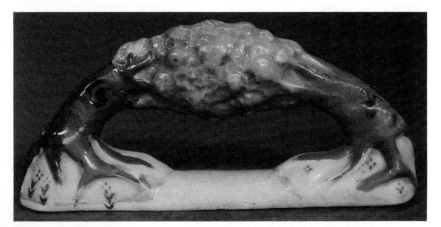

Japanese Tree Bridge, 2 3/4" h - $22

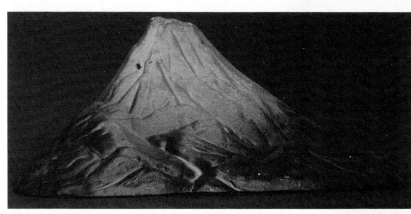

Blue Mountain, Japan, 3" h - $24

Junky Car, 4 3/4" h - $20

Aquarium Miscellaneous

Shell, 1 1/2"h
$12

Coral, 3" h
$22

Viewing Radio, 2 3/4"h
$12

Pink Snail Shell, 2 1/4" h
$10

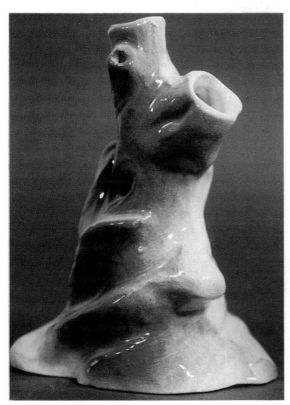

Tree Stump, 7 1/4" h
$22

Skull in middle of Coral,
made in Korea, 9 1/5" h
$26

Aquarium Miscellaneous

Yellow Mushroom, 3 3/4" h
$22

Tree Stamps, 2 1/2" h
$18

Treasure Chest, 1 1/2" h - $22

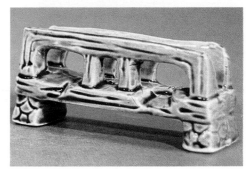

Green Bridge, 1 3/4" h - $18

Sunk Ship, Japan, 2 3/8" h
$24

Trees with barrel, 4 1/4" h
$28

Pirate Hat & Anchor, 2 3/4" h
$24

Palm Tree, Japan, 3 1/2" h
$22

Aquarium Miscellaneous

Dragon, 4 1/2" h
$46

Blue Columns, 3 3/8" h
$26

German Ship, 2 1/2" h
$22

Sail Boat, Japan, 4 1/2" h
$28

Blue Column, 3 3/4" h
$18

Aquarium Miscellaneous

Roman Columns, 4 1/2" h
$26

Colorful Columns, Japan, 4 1/4" h
$34

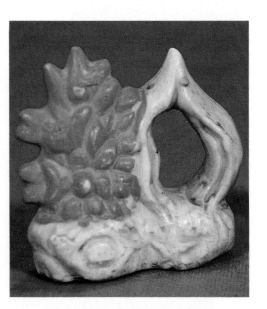

Japanese Plants, 2 3/4" h
$24

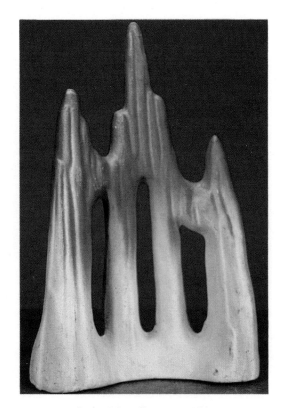

Japan Miscellaneous, 6" h
$26

Kreiss Figurines

Psycho Hound Ashtray, 4 3/4" h
$685

Psycho Personality, 4 7/8" h
$260

Psycho, 4 3/4" h
$975

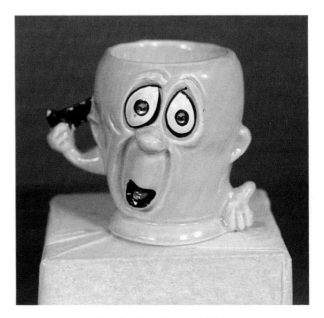

Psycho Egg Cup, 2 1/4" h
$310

Kreiss Figurines

Psychos, No Goodnik & His Helpers,
Left: 4 1/8″ h - $325
Right: 4 3/4″ h - $195

Psycho Figure Ashtray, 4 7/8″ h
$170

Psycho with hair, 5 1/8″ h
$550

Shelf Sitter, 4 3/4″ h
$560

Kreiss Figurines

Psycho, 4 1/4" h
$195

Psycho with hair, 4 7/8" h
$155

Psycho, 5 3/8" h
$220

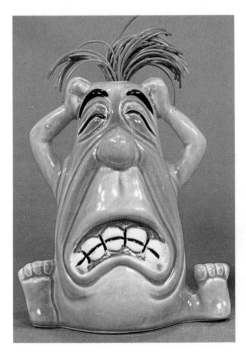

Psycho, 5 1/8" h
$460

Psycho, 5" h
$185

Psycho, 5 1/8" h
$95

Kreiss Figurines

Psycho, 5 7/8″ h
$95

Psycho, 6 5/8″ h
$160

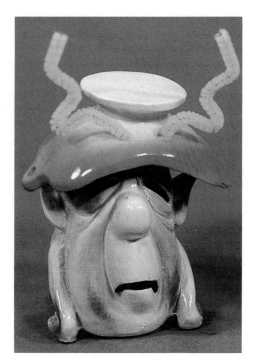

Psycho, 5 1/4″ h
$230

Green-eyed Monster and Friends
Monster is - 6 5/8″ h   Kids are - 3 1/2″ h
$135

Psycho Mug, 4 5/8″ h
$145

Kreiss Figurines

Psycho Christmas, 5 1/2" h
$125

Psycho Christmas, 4 1/4" h
$65

Psycho Christmas, 6 3/4" h
$120

Psycho Christmas
Left: 5 3/8"h - $85
Right: 5 1/2" h - $95

Kreiss Figurines

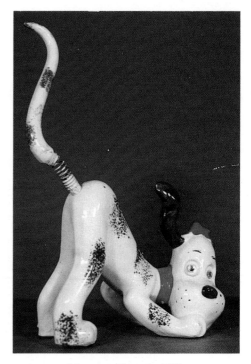

Dog, 4 1/8″ h
$26

Pink Poodle, 6″ tall
$38

Nagging Dog, 6 1/8″ h
$34

Horse, 5 7/8″ h
$42

Cat, 7 3/8″ h
$36

78

Kreiss Figurines

Kreiss Salt & Pepper Shakers, 2 1/2" h
$46

Blue Dr. Seuss like Kreiss figure,
4 1/2" h - $325

Penguins, 3 3/8" h
$28

Left: Kreiss 1957 original tag "Wee Little
Space People", 5 3/4" h - $68

Right: "Wee Little Space People",
5 3/4" h - $68

Nun, 7 1/2" h
$32

Kissing Monkies, 2 3/4" h
$29

Kreiss Figurines

Napkin Lady, 10" h
salt & pepper, 4 7/8" h & 5" h
$145 set

Kreiss Colonial Woman, 8 1/4" h
$72 ea.

Oriental man & woman, 6"h & 5 3/4"h
$26 set

Kreiss Colonial Woman, 8 3/4" h
$56

Kreiss Figurines

Country Boy, 5 3/4" h
$28

Monk, 5 1/2" h
$32

Elegant Heirs
Woman, 6 3/4" h - $110
Man, 6" h - $130

Kreiss Figurines

Colonial Groom, 10 3/4" h
$88

Bouncing Bum
8 7/8" h
$140

Beatchick with base,
7 3/8" h
$160

Beatnik, 3 5/8" h x 6" l
$90

Kreiss Miscellaneous

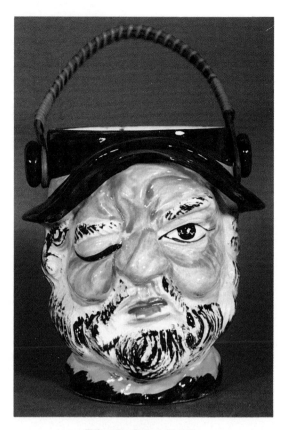

Blue Vase, 7" tall
$68

Vodka Decanter, 12 1/2" h
$86

Toby Cook Jar, 6" tall
(not including handle)
$44

Two Brandy Snifters, each are 6" tall
$58 ea.

Kreiss Miscellaneous

Kreiss Plates
$28 ea

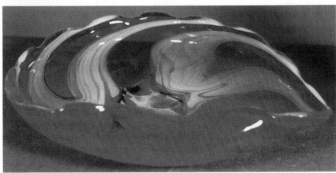

Kreiss Ashtray
2" tall - $38

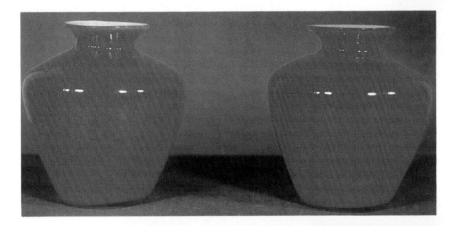

Kreiss Orange Vases
$22 ea

Left: Red Vase, 6 3/4" h - $44
Middle: Orange Vase, 6 1/4" h - $40
Right: Orange Vase, 6 1/4" h - $40

Characters

The Pink Panther, 1981,
4" h - $65

Walt Disney Productions
1982, 3" h
$20

Mammy Dogpatch USA,
1975, Capp Enterprises, Inc.
7 1/4" h - $55

Roadrunner, Warner Bros. Inc.,
1980 CMA Inc., 5 5/8" h
$25

Garfield Figure, 3 1/4" h
$26

Garfield, 1978, 3 3/4" h
$10

Left: "Be My Valentine, I'm All Yours", Garfield, 1981, 3" h - $20
Right: "To Mom . . . from one of the Gang", Garfield, 1978 - $25

"Congratulations" Garfield
Figure, 4 3/4" h
$26

Characters

Mickey Mouse, 6 3/4" h
$40

Left: Bullwinkle, T.M. & Ward Prod., 5" h - $95
Right: Lyle the Lion, 2 1/2" h, Animal Crackers ©
ctnyns. Inc., made in Taiwan. - $20

Left: Jiminy Cricket, Walt Disney Prod., 2 7/8" h - $19
Right: Porky Pig, 4 3/4" h - $45

The Aristocats, Walt Disney
Prod., Japan-Enesco, 1968
4" h - $28

Characters

Raggedy Andy & Ann Planters, 6 5/8" h
$30 ea.

Raggedy Ann & Andy Cat
6 1/2"h - $75

Left: Raggedy Andy, China Novelities, 6 1/2" h - $85
Right: Raggedy Ann's Dog, 6 1/8" h - $85

Characters

Mr. Jinx, 5 1/4" h
$32

Chucky Cheese
Mouse, 4" h
$18

Holly Hobbie made by Stoneware,
Japan, 2 3/16" h
$22

Pillsbury Poppin Fresh Spoon Rest, 1988,
Benjamin & Medwin, Inc., Taiwan - $20

Lewis & Clark Exploration
Gary Schildt, 1970, 13 3/8″ h
$32

Teddy Roosevelt, Grenddier Original,
June 1976, 12 1/4″ h
$55

Characters

The Prairie Dawgs Coll., made by United China & Glass Co.
Left: Deputy-Sheriff Basset, 4 3/4" h - $32
Right: Marshall Mutt, 4 3/4" h - $32

The Prairie Dawgs Coll., made by United China & Glass Co.
Left: Bronco Bully, 5" h - $32
Right: Bulls-eye Blackie, 5" h - $36

The Prairie Dawgs Coll., made by United China & Glass Co.
Left: Pecos Pooch, 4 3/4" h - $38
Right: Wyatt Arf, 4 3/4" h - $38

The Prairie Dawgs Coll., 5 1/4" h
made by United China & Glass Co., Taiwan
$62

The Prairie Dawgs Coll., Music Box,
made by United China & Glass Co.,
Taiwan, 5 1/2" h - $92

The Prairie Dawgs Coll., made by
United China & Glass Co., Taiwan,
4 1/4" h - $62

The Prairie Dawgs Coll., made by
United China & Glass Co., Taiwan,
4 1/4" h - $56

The Prairie Dawgs Coll., that reads "The Branding Time
with Pecos Pooch and Bulls-eye Blackie", 4 3/4" h
$62

Characters

Cathy Figures by George Good Corp., 1982
Left: 4 1/4" h- $55   Right: 3 7/8" h - $32

Cathy Figure, 1982,
4 1/4" h
$42

Cathy Figures by George Good Corp., 1982
Left: 4 5/8"h - $34   Right: 4 5/8" h - $32

Cathy Figures
Left: 4" h - $50   Right: 4 3/4" h - $32

Characters

Left: Cathy Figure by George Good Corp., 1982
4 1/2" h - $32
Right: Cathy Figure by George Good Corp.,
4 9/16" h - $34

Left: Cathy Figure by George Good Corp., 1982
4 1/2" h - $46
Right: Cathy Figure by George Good Corp., 1982
4 2/3" h - $34

Left: Cathy Figure by George Good Corp., 1982
3 3/4" h - $52
Right: Cathy Figure by George Good Corp., 1982
4 1/2" h - $44

Cathy Music Box, 1982,
4 1/8" h - $86

Characters

Cathy Mug, 1995,
Guisewite Studio, 4 1/2" h
$24

Cathy Teapot box, 1995,
7 1/4" h
$46

Cathy Kitchen Collection,
1995, made by Papel in Sr: Lanka,
7 1/8" h - $32

Characters

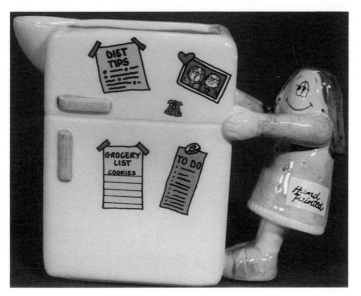

Cathy Creamer
$32

Box for the creamer & sugar bowl
$78 in box

Cathy Sugar Bowl
$30

Ziggy Characters

Ziggy with Butterfly, 3" h
$28

Ziggy, 1982, Earthenware, Taiwan, 6 1/4" h
$48

Ziggy, 1982, Jewelry Box "Spring Love",
Taiwan, 4 1/4" h
$56

Ziggy, 1983, "Lasting Memories", Japan
$20

Ziggy Characters

Ziggy Scratch Pad Holder, 4 1/2" h
$34

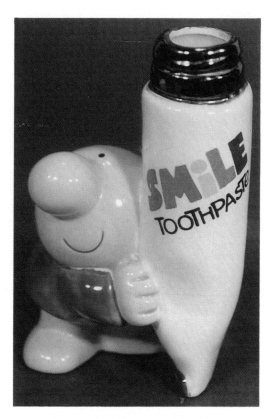

Ziggy, 1982, Toothbrush Holder,
Made by Earthenware, Korea, 5 1/4" h
$67

Ziggy, 1982, Earthenware, Korea, 3 3/4" h
$44

Ziggy, 1982, Earthenware, Korea, 5 1/4" h
$46

Ziggy Characters

Ziggy, 1982, American Greetings, Korea
Left: Chef, 3 1/4" h - $32
Right: Ziggy with bear, 3" h - $26

Left: Ziggy with Pillow, 4" h - $28
Right: Ziggy with Kiss on Head, 3 1/4" h,
      American Greetings, Korea - $26

Left: Ziggy w/clover, made by
      American Greetings, Korea
      1982, 3" h - $26

Right: Ziggy w/Trophy, made by
      American Greetings, Korea
      1982, 2 1/4" h - $24

Ziggy Characters

Ziggy Salt & Pepper Shakers, 1979,
Universal Press Syndicate
$36 pair

Left: Ziggy Paperweight
designer edition, 1980,
2 3/4" h, Japan - $24

Right: Ziggy, American Greetings,
1982, Korea, 2 3/4" h - $26

Left: Ziggy Stoneware, Japan,
2 1/4" h - $32

Right: Ziggy, American Greetings,
Korea, 1992, 3" h - $24

Marvin Characters

Marvin Mug, made by Hallmark, Japan,
1982, 3 6/8" h - $12

Left: Soccer Marvin, 1983, Enesco, 2 7/8" h - $18
Right: Sitting Cute Marvin, 1983, Enesco, 3 1/8" h - $18

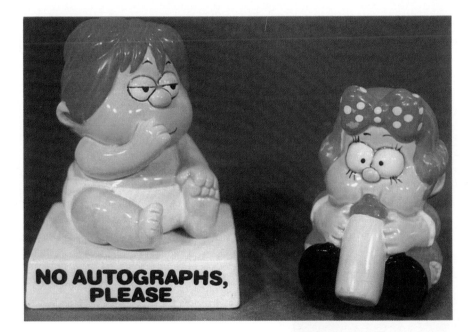

Left: Marvin, 1983, Enesco, 4" h - $22
Right: Marvin's Sister with bottle, 1983,
        Enesco, 3 3/16" h - $20

Left: Marvin crawling, 1983,
        Enesco, 2 1/2" h - $18
Right: Marvin, 1983, Enesco, 2" h - $18

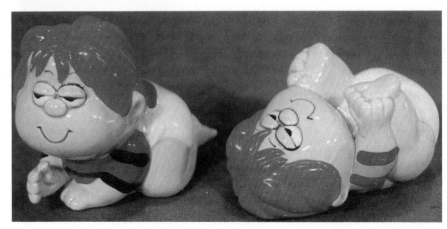

Marvin Characters

Left: Marvin "Beautiful Baby"
        1983, Enesco, 4" h - $22

Right: Marvin's Sister, 1983, Enesco
        3 1/4" h - $20

Left: Marvin with Sunglasses
        1983, Enesco, 4" h - $22

Right: Marvin's Sister, 1983, Enesco
        3 1/4" h - $20

Left: Marvin, 1983, Enesco,
        made in Korea, 3" h - $18

Right: "Baby Face" Marvin, 1983,
        Enesco, Korea, 4 1/4" h - $22

Marvin Characters

Left: Marvin with Wreath
1983, Enesco, 3" h - $20

Right: Marvinwith Christmas Blocks,
1983, Enesco, 3 1/4" h - $22

Left: Christmas List Marvin,
1983, Enesco, 3 1/4" h - $22

Right: Marvinwith Blocks,
1983, Enesco, 4 1/2" h - $24

Marvin, Enesco, Korea,
6 1/4" h - $48

Annie Characters

Annie, by Applause,
Japan, 5" h - $48

Annie and Sandy, by Applause,
Japan, 5 3/8" h - $48

Annie, by Applause, Japan,
1982, 4 1/8" h - $46

Annie and Sandy Bank, by Applause,
Japan, 1982, 6 7/8" h - $46

Annie, made by Applause, Japan,
1982, 4" h - $46

Annie, by Applause, made in Japan,
1982, 4" h - $46

Miscellaneous Characters

Pound Puppies, 1985-86, Tonka Corp.
United Silver Cutlery Co.
Left: Cooler, 3 7/8" h - $25
Right: Bright Eyes, 4" h - $25

Piggy from Muppets
by Sigma, 7 1/2" h
$46

Get Along Gang, American Greeting Corp.
1984, 5 7/8"h, Music Box - $70

Pound Puppies, 1986, Tonka Corp. United Silver & Cutlery Co.
Left: Howler, 1985, Tonka, 4" h - $25
Right: Rose Marie, 1985, Tonka, 3 3/4" h - $25

Dear God Kids

Dear God Kids, 1982, Enesco
Left: Rainbow, 3 1/2" h - $36
Right: Bookshelf, 3 3/4" h - $28

Dear God Kids, 1982, Licensee Enesco
Left: Rainbow, 3 1/4" h - $36
Right: Famous Book, 4 3/4" h - $28

Dear God Kids, Enesco
Left: 1982, 4" h - $28
Right: 1983, 3 1/2" h - $38

Dear God Kids, 1982, Enesco
Left: 3 1/4" h - $26
Right: 3 3/8" h - $26

Dear God Kids

Dear God Kids, 1982, Enesco, 3 1/2" h
$38

Dear God Kids, 1982, Enesco, 3 1/2" h
$42

Dear God Kids, Intercontinental
Licensee Enesco
Left: 1982, 3 1/2" h - $26
Right: 1983, 3 5/8" h - $12

Dear God Kids, 1982,
Intercontinental Enesco
Left: 3 1/2" h - $42
Right: 3" h - $29

Dear God Kids

Dear God Kids, 1982, Enesco,
3 3/4" h - $40

Dear God Kids, 1982, Enesco, 3 1/4" h
$38

Dear God Kids, Enesco, 1982
Left: 3" h - $32
Right: Bank, 5 1/2" h - $48

Dear God Kids, 1982, 3 1/4" h
Intercontinental Licensee Enesco
$32

Dear God Kids, 1982, Enesco, Both are 3 1/2" h
Left: $38   Right: $36

Dear God Kids

Dear God Kids
3" h - $25

Dear God Kids, 1982, Enesco
Left: 4 1/4" h - $34
Right: 3 7/8" h - $34

Dear God Kids, Enesco
Left: 1982, 4 1/4" h - $38
Right: 1983, 3 3/4" h - $34

Dear God Kids, Enesco,
1982, 3 1/4" h - $32

Dear God Kids, 1982, Enesco,
2 1/2" h - $18

Dear God Kids, made in Korea by Enesco, 1982
Left: 3 1/2" h - $22
Right: 3 1/4" h - $36

Dear God Kids

Dear God Kids, 1982, Enesco
Left: 3 1/4" h - $34
Right: 4 3/4" h - $34

Dear God Kids, 1982,
Enesco, 2 3/4" h
$25

Dear God Kids, Enesco
Left: 1983, 3" h - $36
Right: 1982, 2 1/2" L - $18

Dear God Kids Bank, made in Korea by Enesco,
1982, 5 3/4" h - $48

Dear God Kids, Enesco
Left: 1982, 4 1/4" h - $38
Right: 1983, 4 1/2" h - $38

Dear God Kids

Dear God Kids, Wedding Cake Topper,
Music Box, 1982m, Enesco, Korea, 4 3/4" h
$92

Dear God Kids Music Box, made in Korea
by Enesco, 5 1/2" h - $92

Dear God Kids Cookie Jar, 1983,
Enesco, 8" h - $94

Dear God Kids Utensil Holder, 1982,
Intercontinental Enesco, 6 1/2" h - $80

111

General Human Beans

Acrobat Human Beans Bank
$140

Birthday Human Bean, 1983,
Enesco, 3" h - $26

Grandfather Human
Bean, 1981, 2" h
$20

Left: Happy Birthday Human Bean, 3 1/4" h - $22
Middle: Baby Me Human Bean, Enesco, 1981, 2 3/4" h - $22
Right: Celebrate Human Bean, Enesco, 3 1/4" h - $22

General Human Beans

Circumstance Human Bean,
1981, 3" h - $26

Left: Graduate Human Bean, 1983, 3 1/8" h - $26
Right: Glad Grad Human Bean, 1981, 3" h - $26

Moms are Special Human Bean
1981, 4" h, Srilanka
$30

Left: Grandma Human Bean,
1981, Enesco, 4 1/4" h - $26

Right: Grandpa Human Bean,
1981, Enesco, 4" h - $26

General Human Beans

Left: Thank You Human
Bean, 4 1/8″ h, 1981 - $26

Right: I Miss You Human Bean
1981, 4″ h - $26

Left: Human Bean, 1981,
Enesco, 4 1/4″ h - $28

Right: Spring Human Bean, 1981
Enesco, 4 1/4″ h - $26

Human Beans, 1981, Enesco
Left: 3 3/4″ h - $26
Right: 4″ h - $26

General Human Beans

Human Bean Key Chains
1981, both are 1 1/2" h
$15 ea.

Human Beans, 1981,
Enesco, both are 4" h
$26 ea.

Leprechaun Human Beans
1981, Enesco
Left: 4 1/2" h - $28
Right: 4 3/8" h - $28

Human Bean Mugs & Dishes

Human Bean Mug, 3 1/2" h
Enesco - $15

Human Bean Mugs,
1981, both are 3 3/8" h
$15 ea.

Human Bean Mugs
1981, Enesco, 3 1/2" h
$15 ea.

Human Bean Mugs & Dishes

Human Bean Lovable Mug, 1981,
Morgan Inc., Enesco, 4" h - $26

Human Bean Mug, 1981,
Morgan Inc., Enesco, 4" h - $26

Left: Human Bean Plate, 1981, Enesco, 7" h - $15
Right: Human Bean Cup, 1981, Enesco, 3 1/8" h - $15

Professional Human Beans

Secretary Human Bean, 1981, 4" h
$28

Teacher Human Bean, 1981,
Sri Lanka, 4 1/4" h - $28

Monk Human Bean, 1981, 3" h
$26

Teacher Human Bean, 1981, 2 3/4" h
$28

Nurse Human Bean,
1981, 4 1/8" h
$28

Executive Human Bean,
1981, 3 3/4" h
$28

Professional Human Beans

Left: Mailman Human Bean
1981, 2 3/4" h - $24

Right: Policeman Human Bean
1981, 3" h - $24

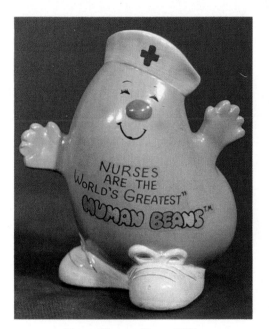

Nurse Human Bean, 1981,
Sri Lanka, 4" h - $28

Nurse Human Bean, 1981, 4 1/8" h
$28

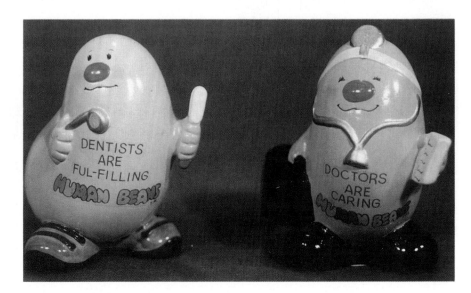

Left: Dentist Human Bean
1981, 3 3/4" h - $28

Right: Doctor Human Bean
1981, 4" h - $28

Human Bean Banks

Human Bean Bank, 5 3/4" h
$35

Christmas Santa and Kid Human Bean, Bank,
1981, Enesco, 4 3/4" h - $35

Retired Human Beans
1981, 5 3/4" h
$35 ea.

Egg Bank, 1982, Enesco, 4 1/4" h
$30

Bowling Human Bean Bank, 1981,
Enesco, 5 3/4" h - $35

Human Bean Banks

Tennis Human Bean Bank,
1981, Enesco, 6 1/4" h
$38

Human Bean Bank, Enesco, 5 3/4" h
$35

Nurse Human Bean Bank,
Enesco, 5 1/2" h
$35

Snow Skier Human Bean Bank,
1981, 7 1/8" h
$40

Human Bean Kitchenware

Christmas Human Bean Jelly Bean Jar,
1981, Enesco, 7" h
$56

Chef Human Bean Utensil Holder,
1981, Enesco, 6 1/2" h
$70

Human Bean Cookie Jar,
1981, Enesco, 8 3/4" h
$180

Human Beans, Jelly Bean Containers,
1981, 6" h - $48 ea.

Human Bean Band Members

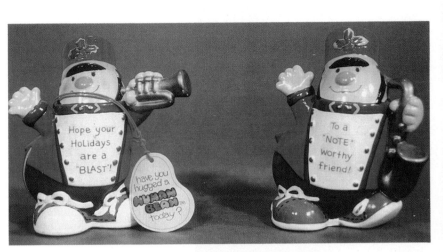

Marching Band Human Beans, 1981, Enesco
Left: Trumpet player, 4 3/8" h - $32
Right: Saxophone player, 4 1/2" h - $32

Human Bean Drummer Bank,
1981, Enesco, 6 2/3" h
$42

Marching Band Human Beans, 1981, Enesco
Left: Cymbal player, 4 1/2" h - $32
Right: Drummer, 5" h - $32

Marching Band Human Beans, 1981, Enesco
Left: Flute player, 4 1/2" h - $32
Right: Band Leader, 4 1/2" h - $32

Non-Ceramic Human Beans

Human Beans, stuffed,
1980, Enesco
Left: 4 3/4" h - $12
Right: 4 1/2" h - $12

Human Beans, stuffed,
1980, Enesco
Left: 3 1/2" h - $12
Right: 3 3/4" h - $12

Human Beans, stuffed,
1981, Enesco
Left: 5" h - $12
Right: 3 1/2" h - $12

Non-Ceramic Human Beans

Human Bean, stuffed, Enesco, 1982, 11 1/8" h
$24

Human Bean Key Rings, 7"h and the figure is 2 1/2" h
$10

Human Bean Buttons
Left: the card is 5 1/8" h and the figure is 2 1/4" h
Right: the card is 5 1/8"h and the figure is 2" h
$10 each

Human Bean Button,
5 1/8" h
$10

Non-Ceramic Human Beans

Human Bean Plaques
1981, Enesco, 4 1/4″ x 4 1/2″
$15 ea.

Human Bean Plaques
1981, Enesco, 4 1/4″ x 4 1/2″
$15 ea.

Human Bean Plaques
1981, Enesco, 4 1/4″ x 4 1/2″
$15 ea.

Non-Ceramic Human Beans

Human Bean Plaques
1981, Enesco, 4 1/4" x 4 1/2"
$15 ea.

Human Bean Plaques
1981, Enesco, 4 1/4" x 4 1/2"
$15 ea.

Human Bean Plaques
1981, Enesco, 4 1/4" x 4 1/2"
$15 ea.

Easter Human Beans

Human Beans, 1981,
Enesco, 3 1/8"h ea.
Left: $34   Right: $34

Human Beans, 1981, Enesco
Left: 4 1/8" h - $34
Right: 4 3/4" h - $34

Human Beans, 1981, Enesco
Left: Jelly Bean Container,
4 1/8" h - $34
Right: 4 1/8" h - $34

Valentine Human Beans

Human Bean, 1981, 4 1/8" h
$28

Human Bean, 1981, 2 3/4" h
$24

Human Bean, 1981, 4" h
$28

Human Bean, 4" h - $28

Human Beans, 1981
Left: 4 1/8" h - $28   Right: 4 1/4" h - $28

Human Beans, 1981
Left: 3" h - $24   Right: 3 1/8" h - $24

Human Bean, 4 1/4" h - $28

Christmas Human Beans

Bell, 1981, Enesco, 6" h - $46

Christmas Human Bean Music Box - $135

Human Bean Skater, 3 1/2" h - $26

Human Bean, Enesco, 3 1/4" h
$26

Human Beans, 1981
Left: 3 3/4" h - $34
Right: 4 3/8" h - $34

Christmas Human Beans

Left: Human Bean Skater,
1981, 4 1/4" h - $28

Right: Grandpa Christmas
Human Bean, 1981,
4 1/8" h - $28

Left: Christmas Human
Bean, 1981, Enesco,
4 1/8" h - $28

Right: Christmas Human
Bean Bank, 3 1/4" h
$26

Left: Human Bean Santa,
3" h - $26

Right: Human Bean Mrs. Claus
2 3/4" h - $26

Christmas Human Beans

Left: Christmas Human Bean, 1981, 3 1/8" h $26

Right: St. Patrick Human Bean, 1981, 3" h - $26

Left: Human Bean Skier, 1981, Enesco, 4 1/4" h - $32

Right: Snowman Human Bean, 1981, 4 1/8" h - $28

Left: Christmas Human Bean, Sri Lanka, 1981, 3 1/8" h $26

Right: Christmas Human Bean, Sri Lanka, 1981, 4 1/8" h $28

Christmas Human Beans

Bowling Human Bean, 1981
4 1/4" h - $28

Baseball Human Bean, 1981
4" h - $28

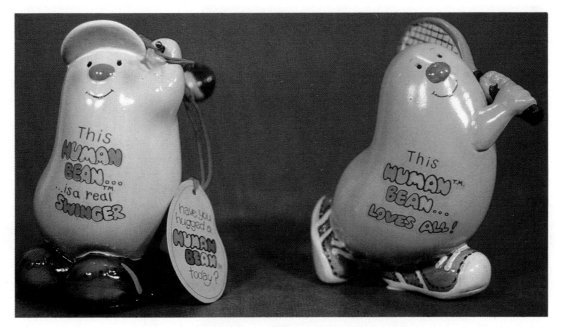

Left: Golfer Human Bean, 1981, 4 1/4" h - $28
Right: Tennis Human Bean, 1981, 4 1/4" h - $28

Miscellaneous Ashtrays

Prunk Ashtray, 6 3/8" h
$45

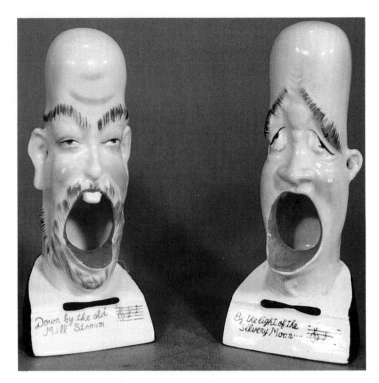

Singing Man Ashtrays - $65 ea.
Left: 5 1/8" h   Right: 5 1/2" h

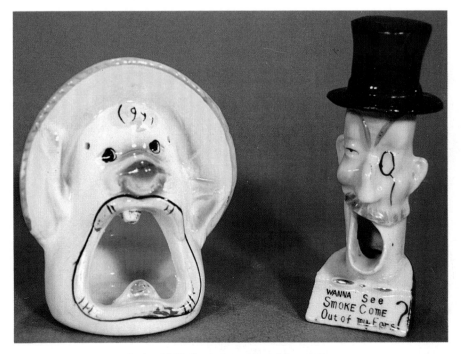

Left: Hillbilly Ashtray, 4 1/8" h - $45
Right: Man in Top Hat Ashtray, 4 1/2" h - $55

Sheriff Ashtray, Japan, 5 7/16" h
$65

Miscellaneous Ashtrays

Howard Holt Ashtray - $60

Hunter Ashtray, Enesco, Japan, 5 3/8" h - $45

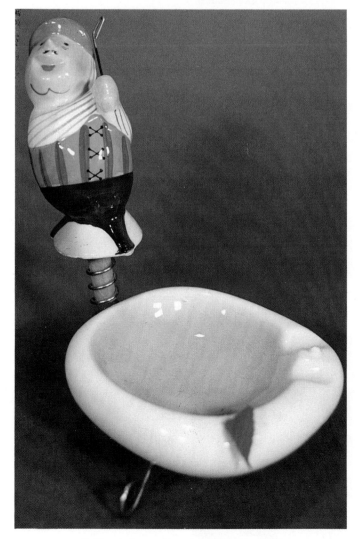

Golfer Ashtray, Enesco, 6 1/4" h - $45

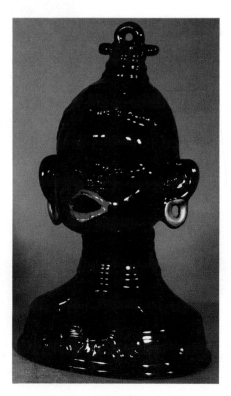

Native Ashtray, Japan, 8" h
$55

Miscellaneous Ashtrays

Left: Clown Smoker
        Cigarette Holder,
        4 1/8" h - $44

Right: The Sympathetic Ear,
        1958, Art Anson Inc.
        6 1/2" h - $56

Left: Snake Ashtray,
        2 1/2" h - $35

Right: Snake Ashtray, 2" h - $26

Snake Ashtrays, 3" h - $35 ea.

Miscellaneous Ashtrays

George Hessberg Restaurant Ashtray, 3 1/2" h - $35

Boot Hill Ashtray, 4 1/2" h - $35

Ashtray, 1952, marked JH Fuller, 3 1/2" h - $45

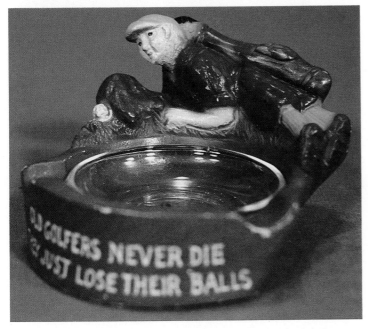

Golfer Ashtray, 1952, marked JH Fuller, 2 1/2" h - $45

Ashtray, 1952, marked JH Fuller, 3" h - $45

Miscellaneous Ashtrays

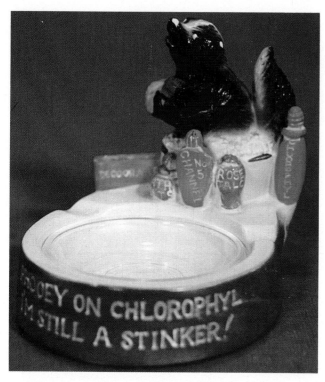

Skunk Ashtray, 1952,
marked JH Fuller, 3 3/4" h
$45

Ashtray, 1952, marked JC Larsen,
4 1/4" h - $45

Ashtray, 1952, marked JC Larsen,
5" h - $45

Ashtray, 1952, marked JH Fuller,
3 5/8" h - $45

Miscellaneous Ashtrays

Ashtray, 3 3/4" h - $45

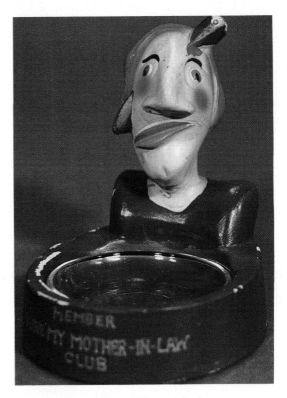

Ashtray, 1952, marked
JC Larsen, 4 3/4" h - $45

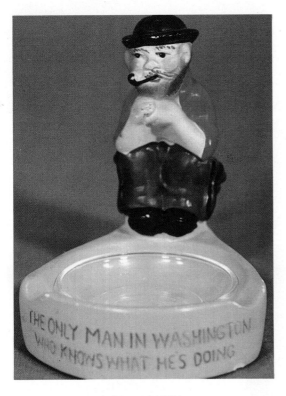

Ashtray, 4 1/2" h,
marked JH Fuller - $45

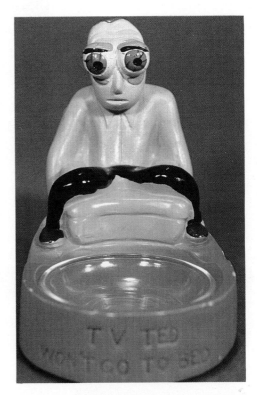

Ashtray, 1952, 4 3/4" h,
marked JC Larsen - $45

Miscellaneous Ashtrays

Ashtray, 1952,
marked O. Bevere,
2 1/4" h - $45

Ashtray, 1951, 2 1/4" h,
marked JH Fuller
$45

Ashtray, 1951, 3 1/4" h,
marked JH Fuller
$45

Miscellaneous Banks

Poodle Bank and Letter Holder, 7 1/2" h
$75

Skunk Bank, 5 3/4" h
$32

Squirrel Bank, 5 3/4" h - $32

Boy Bank, 6 3/8" h - $35

Baby's First Bank, 4 1/2" h - $30

Miscellaneous Banks

Indian Bank, Japan, 6 3/4" h - $42

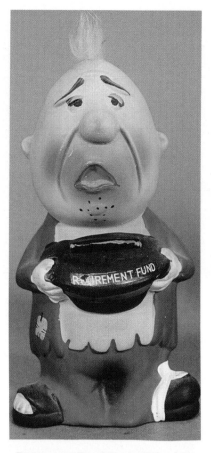

Retirement Fund Bank, 7" h - $42

Stock Market Investor Bank, 6 3/4" h
$42

Bank, 6 1/2" h - $42

Miscellaneous Banks

Left: Mad Money Bank, 6 3/4" h - $42
Right: Dog Bank, 5 3/8" h - $46

Midget Bank, 10" h
$36

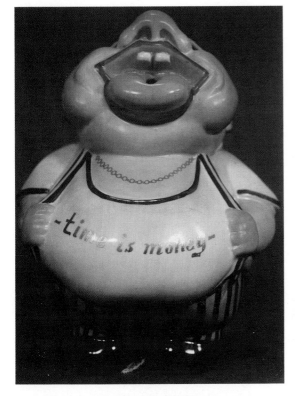

Fat Man Bank, 8" h
$65

Left: Soccer Boy, 5 7/8" h - $38
Right: Elephant, 5 7/8" h - $36

Miscellaneous Banks

Dragon Bank, 8" h
$55

Left: Santa Bank, 6 1/2" h - $68
Right: Hobo Bank, 7" h - $42

Left: Leprechaun with pot of gold,
        7 1/2" h, Marika's Original - $48
Right: Retirement Fund Bank, 6 3/4" h - $32

Grandpa & Baby Bank,
8 5/8" h - $48

Miscellaneous Figures

Luster Boy, 3 1/2" h
$65

Bunny Daffy Bell, 4 3/4" h, Japan
$55

Big Chief's Cigar Holder,
5 7/8" h - $55

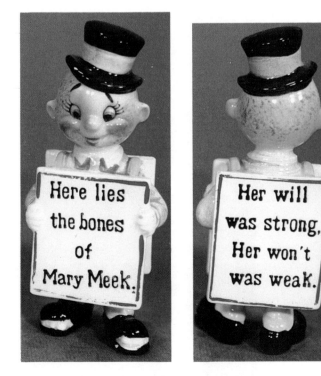

Front and back view of a
Man holding a Mary Meek Sign,
4 1/2" h - $26

Front and back view of a
Man holding a Marriage Partnership Sign,
4 1/2" h - $26

Miscellaneous Figures

Congratulations, 6 1/8" h
$32

Man with Braces,
4 1/2" h - $32

Planter, Japan,
5 1/2" h - $32

Brother Juniper, 1960,
Publishing Syndicate,
by the Shafford Co.,
4 1/4" h - $45

Hobo Clown Arnartcreation,
Japan, 7 1/4" h - $52

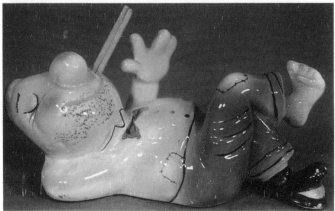

Smoker, Norcrest, 2 1/2" h - $26

Miscellaneous Figures

Natives, Japan
Left: 6 1/2" h - $62   Right: 6 3/8" h - $58

Natives, Pal Mar, Japan
Left: 5 1/2" h - $56   Right: 6" h - $58

Napco Sheriff, Japan
Left: 8" h - $48   Right: 5 1/2" - $42

Left: School Boy, 5 1/4" h - $28
Right: Silver Knight, 5" - $28

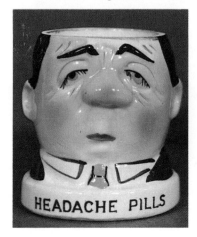

Headache Pills Cup, 1960,
Shafford Co., 2 3/4" h - $25

Left: Baby King, 4 3/4" h - $38
Middle: Fresh Air Sprite, 4 1/4" h - $36
Right: Baby Queen, 4 3/4" - $38

Miscellaneous Figures

Mermaid in Shell, 4" h - $38

Left: Liquor Man, 5 3/4" h - $32
Right: Doctor, 6 1/4" h - $30

Left to Right: Bum and a Swami
6 1/4" h - $40 ea.

The Happy Friars - $36 ea.
Left: Goodwill, 6 1/4"   Right: Candle Holder 6 1/4"   Left: Short, 5 1/2"   Right: Nosey, 6 1/2"

Miscellaneous Figures

Chef, 5" h - $24

Left: Sorry Guy, Enesco, 4 3/4" h - $26
Right: Let's Split, Enesco, 5" h - $26

Left: Side by Side, Enesco, 4 1/4" h - $26
Right: TNT Doctor, Enesco, 4 3/4" h - $26

The Boxer, 5" h - $28

Left: Candleholder, 1958, Holt Howard, Japan, 3 1/2" h - $28
Right: Lining Up Golfer, Dave Grossman Designs, Inc., 1978, 3 1/4" h - $28

Miscellaneous Figures

Alter Egos, 1959, Japan
Left: 5 1/4" h Mid Left: 3" h - $34
Right: 5 1/4" h Mid Right: 3" h - $34

The Tennis Player,
4 3/4" h - 28

Drunk Girl, Enesco, Japan,
4 3/4" h - $22

Alter Egos, 1959, Shafford, Japan
All are 5 1/4" & 3" h - $34 ea. set

Alter Egos, 1959,
Shafford, Japan
All are 5 1/4" & 3" h
Left figs: $34   Right figs: $34

Miscellaneous Figures

Alter Egos, 1959, Shafford, Japan
5 1/4" & 3" h - $34

Alter Egos, 1959, Shafford, Japan
All are 5 1/4" & 3" h
Left figs: $36   Right figs: $34

Alter Egos, 1959, Shafford, Japan
All are 5 1/4" & 3" h - $34 ea. set

Perfect Sports, 1959, Shafford, Japan,
both are 5 1/4" h - $34 ea.

Miscellaneous Figures

Pro Golf Perfect Sports, 1959,
Shafford, Japan, 5" h - $34

Fisherman Perfect Sport Series,
5" h - $34

Fisherman, 5 1/2" h - $38

Left: Golfer, Enesco, Japan, 5 1/2" h - $44
Right: Fisherman, Enesco, Japan, 5 3/4" h - $44

Left: Hunter, Enesco, Japan, 5 3/4" h - $44
Right: Middle Age Pro, Enesco, Japan, 5 1/2" h - $44

Miscellaneous Figures

Left: Pitcher, Enesco, 5 3/4" h - $44
Right: Batter, Enesco, 5 3/4" h - $44

Left: Man with Ladder, Enesco, Japan, 6" h - $44
Right: Man with Paint, Enesco, Japan, 5 3/4" h - $44

Left: Golfer, Enesco,
         5 3/4" h - $44

Right: Boy & Girl,
         3 3/4" h - $28 set

Left: Chef, 5 1/2" h - $44
Right: Tennis Pro, 1978, 5" h,
       Dave Grossman Designs, Inc. - $32

Golfer, Napcoware, Japan, 5 5/8" h
$38

Miscellaneous Figures

Graduate, Kelvin Exclusive, 1961
3 3/4" h - $38

King & Queen Egg Holders, 5 3/4" h
$41 ea.

Left: Green Elf, 4 1/4" h - $26
Right: Elves, 3 1/2" l - $26

Left: Girl in Pink Shirt, Norcrest, Japan, 5" h - $32
Right: Girl in Green Skirt, Norcrest, Japan, 5" h - $32

Left: Girl, 5 1/4" h - $32
Right: Boy, 5 1/4" h - $32

Miscellaneous Figures

Hobo with umbrella,
8 3/4" h - $24

Left: Hobo with whiskey and
        brown hat, 8 3/4" h - $24
Right: Hobo with cane and blue
        hat, 8 3/4" h - $24

Thermo Man, 8" h - $44

Left: Hobo, 6 3/4" h - $24
Right: Hobo, 5 1/4" h - $20

Left: Caveman, 4 3/4" h - $28
Right: Man in a blue suit, 5" h - $26

Miscellaneous Figures

Left: Caveman, 5" h - $28
Right: Caveman, 5 1/4" h - $28

Left: Caveman, 4 1/4" h - $28
Right: Elves, 3" h - $22

Left: Caveman, 4 1/4" h - $28
Right: Caveman, 5" h - $28

Left: Caveman, 6" h - $28
Right: Caveman, 6" h - $28

Miscellaneous Figures

Clown Decanter, Italy, 12" h
$96

Clown Decanter, Italy, 12" h
$96

Left: Hobo, Enesco,
        4 1/4" h - $26
Right: Diamond in Rough,
        Enesco, 5" h - $26

Diamond in the Rough Characters,
Enesco, grey suit, 4 1/2" h
black 4 3/4" h
$26

Miscellaneous Figures

Cute No Matter What Figure,
Enesco, Sri Lanka, 4" h
$38

Chef and Baby Little Darling,
Enesco, Sri Lanka, 4 1/4" h
$38

Little Darling, 1982, Enesco, Sri Lanka, 4 1/4" h
$38

Mommy and Baby Little Darling,
Enesco, Sri Lanka
$38

Miscellaneous Figures

Left: Adorables, 4 1/2" h - $22
Right: Adorables, 4 3/4" h - $22

Adorables, 4 1/2" h
$22

Left: Adorables, 4 1/2" h - $22
Right: Adorables, 4 1/2" h - $22

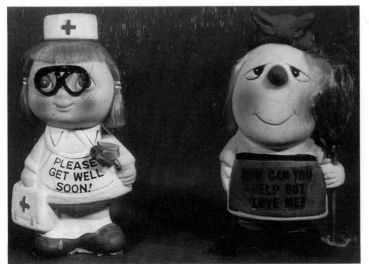

Left: Nurse, 4 3/4" h - $26
Right: Maid, Enesco, 4 1/2" h - $26

Weird Miscellaneous Figures

Left: Woman with mop, Norcrest, Japan, 8" h - $48
Right: Woman with head underfoot, Norcrest, Japan, 8" h - $48

Robots
Left: 8 1/2" h - $48   Right: 6 1/4" h - $36

Clever Man Figurine, Norcrest, Japan, 6 1/2" h - $36 ea

Middle Picture:
Clever Man, Norcrest, Schilo Ceramics, 8 1/4" h - $48

Trash Can Bum, 6" h
$36

Weird Miscellaneous Figures

Cavemen, 6" h - $38 ea.

Cup with Man for Handle,
by Wales, Japan, 5 1/2" h - $25

Forgive Me Figure,
$28

Undertaker and Wife Salt & Pepper Shakers
$45 set

Astronaut Salt & Pepper Shakers, 3 1/4" h
$45

Weird Miscellaneous Figures

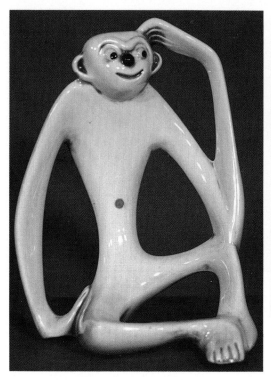

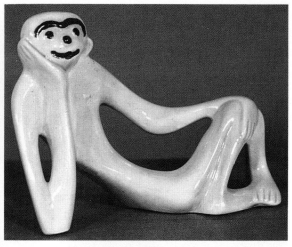

Monkey, 4" h - $28

Bum, 4" h
$25

Monkey Man, 6 1/4" h - $28

Tickle Me, 3 3/4" h - $32

Sword Swallower, Japan,
5" h - $32

El Dera - $26 ea.
Left: 5 3/4" h   Right: 4" h

Weird Miscellaneous Figures

Pencil Sharpener, Lugenes, Japan,
4 3/4" h - $35

Here's lookin at Yuh Plate,
Japan, 1 3/8" h
$25

You carry your age so well Figure with original box.
$36

Winner, Japan, 5 1/4" h - $44

Weird Miscellaneous Figures

Pencil Holder, 4 3/4" h - $22

Left: Woman in blue dress, 4 3/4" h - $36
Right: Woman in pink dress, 4 3/4" h - $36

Left: Man in blue suit, Japan, 4 1/2" h - $36
Right: Woman in red dress, 4 3/4" h - $36

Astronaut, 4 1/2" h - $44

Man with red Toenails,
4 1/2" h - $36

Left: Cross Eyed Monster, 4 3/4" h - $ 42
Right: Blue Eyed Monster, 5" h - $42

Left: Worry Bird, blue, 5" h - $28
Right: Worry Bird, red, , 5" h - $28

Weird Miscellaneous Figures

Dentist, 5 1/2" h - $34

Left: Happy Birthday Figure, 6 1/8" h - $38
Right: Happy Birthday Figure, 6" h - $38

The Pupies, Enesco
Imports Japan, 5 1/2" h
$44 ea.

Bikini Figure, 4" h - $42

Men Figures, Japan
Left: 5 1/8" h - $64
Right: 5" h - $64

Weird Miscellaneous Figures

Mirror Man, by Wales, Japan, 5 1/4" h - $64

Man Figure, by
Wales, Japan, 6 1/4" h
$85

Man with Big Mouth, by Wales, Japan,
5 1/2" h - $64

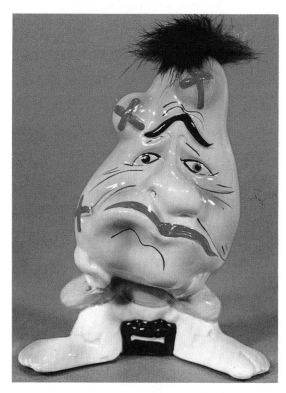

Head Bumps, 5 1/4" h - $64

Left: Man with rope, by Wales, Japan, 6" h - $85
Right: Man with no Shoes, by Wales, Japan, 6 1/8" h - $85

Weird Miscellaneous Figures

Left: Sitting Man, by Wales, Japan, 6" h - $85
Right: Standing Man, by Wales, Japan, 6 3/4" h - $85

Man on Scales, 4 1/2" h - $40

Prisioners of Love
Left: 6 1/2" h - $46   Right: 5" h - $36

Men Figures, by Wales, Japan
Left: 6 1/4" h - $85   Right: 6" h - $85

Weird Miscellaneous Figures

Left: Some Wives Will Kill You, by Wales, Japan, 5 3/4" h - $85
Right: Toliet Man, by Wales, Japan, 6" h - $120

Left: Square Figure, by Lipper & Mann, Inc.
Japan, 6 3/5" h - $42
Right: Beatnik, by Riese, Japan, 6 7/10" h - $42

Let's Put Our Heads Together Figurine,
by Vcagco, Japan - $46

Egg Heads Figures, by Chase Import, Japan, 6 1/4" h
Left: $56   Right: $56

Left: Hippie Guitarist, by Napco,
6" h - $36
Right: Hippie Protester, by Napco,
5 3/4" h - $36

Weird Miscellaneous Figures

Left: Take Me Seriously, by Vcagco,
Japan, 5 3/8" h - $44
Right: Tip of My Tounge, by Vcagco,
Japan, 5 3/4" h - $44

Left: Under My Skin, by Vcagco, Japan, 5 6/8" h - $44
Right: Travel Bradens, by Vcagco, Japan, 4 3/4" h - $44

Left: I Dig You the Most, by Vcagco,
Japan, 4 3/4" h - $46
Right: Ear for Music, by Vcagco,
Japan, 5 3/4" h - $44

Left: Slob Figure, 5 1/4" h - $28
Right: Perfect Sports, 1959,
by Shafford, Japan, 5 1/2" h - $34

Weird Miscellaneous Figures

Left: Man at the Gas Pump, 1979,
Enesco, 3 1/2" h - $38
Right: Lady at the Gas Pump, 1979,
Enesco, 3 1/2" h - $38

Left: Cowboy at the Gas Pump,
1979, Enesco, 3 1/2" h - $38
Right: Pregnant Lady at the Gas
Pump, Enesco, 3 1/2" h - $38

Left: Man with a gun at the Gas Pump, 1979,
Enesco, 3 1/2" h - $38
Right: Lady at the Gas Pump, 1979, Enesco, 3 1/2" h - $38

Rooster Shakers, by Holt Howard, 4 3/4" h - $36

Filler Up Bank, Enesco, Japan, 6 3?10" h
$48

Miscellaneous Salt & Pepper Shakers

Left: Salt & Pepper, Japan
3"h & 3 1/2" h - $68

Right: Bear Shakers, by Ceramic
Arts Studios, Salt 2 1/4" h
Pepper 4 1/4"h - $44

Salt & Pepper Shakers,
Japan, 3" h - $68 set

Chef Shakers,
3 1/2" h - $45

Miscellaneous Salt & Pepper Shakers

Salt & Pepper Shakers, Japan - $68 set
Left: 3" h   Right: 3 1/2" h

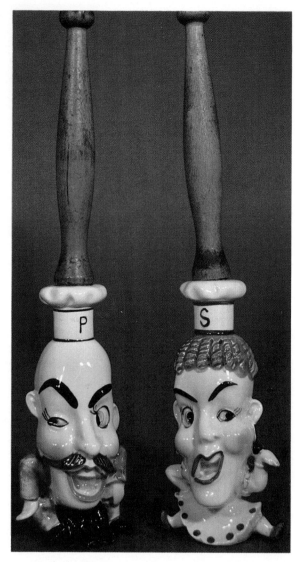

Man and Woman Shakers, 10 1/2" h - $56 set

Salt and Pepper Shakers, Japan,
3 1/2" h - $68 set

Shakers, 4" h - $22 ea.

Miscellaneous Salt & Pepper Shakers

Shakers, 3" h & 3 1/2" h - $68 set

Donkey Shakers, 4" h - $32 set

Left: Lady & The Tramp
Shakers, 3" h &
3 3/4" h - $65
Right: Disney's Pluto
Shakers 2 1/2" h &
3 1/2" h - $55

Miscellaneous Salt & Pepper Shakers

Puppy Shakers, Lefton
Trademark Exclusives, Japan,
3 1/4" h - $28

Christmas Puppy Shakers,
Lefton, Japan, 3 1/2" h &
3 1/4" h - $26 set

Man and Woman with Stump
Salt and Pepper Shakers,
3 1/2" h - $44

Miscellaneous Dresser Caddys

Black Dog Dresser Caddy, 4 1/2" h - $35

Hobo Dresser Caddy, Japan, 10" h
$35

Dachshund Dresser Caddy,
Japan, 5 1/4" h - $35

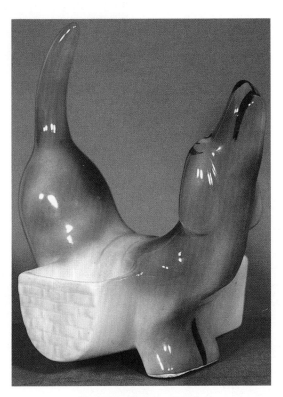

Red Dog Dresser Caddy
$35

Miscellaneous Odds & Ends

Jester Cream Pitcher,
England, 3 1/4" h - $55

Figural Cream Pitcher,
Japan, 3 1/4" h - $55

Left: Castle Incense Burner, 6 3/4" h - $54
Right: Cottage Incense Burner, 6 3/4" h - $54

Cottage Incense Burner,
4" h, Japan - $54

Incense Burner, Japan, 5 1/2" h - $54

Miscellaneous Animals

Left: The Golfer, 5 1/8" h - $28
Right: The Dreamer, 4 2/3" h - $28

The Barber, Japan, 4 3/4" h
$28

Left: The Golfer, 5 1/8" h - $28
Right: The Dreamer, 4 2/3" h - $28

Dolphin, 3 1/4" h - $55

Donkey, 4" h - $20

Left: The Playboy, Japan, 5 1/4" h - $28
Right: Our Leader, Japan, 5" h - $28

Miscellaneous Animals

Left: The Cook, Japan, 5" h - $28
Right: Ladies Man, Japan, 5 1/8" h - $28

Dirty Dog Series, 1973, Japan,
by World Wide, 5 7/8" h - $45

Mothers Helper, by
Vcagco, Japan, 6 1/2" h
$28

Horse with spring tail and head, 4 1/2" h - $38

Kitty, 4 1/4" h - $20

Left: Germany Luster Pup,
          2 1/2" h - $27
Right: Scottish Dog, Japan,
          3" h - $26

Miscellaneous Animals

Playful Cats - $22 ea.
Left: 2 13/16" h   Right: 2 1/4" h

Dirty Dogs Series, 1973, by World Wide Arts, Japan - $45 ea.
Left: 6 1/5" h   Right: 6" h

Look out for temptations— or you might miss some!

When you got it... flaunt it!

Black Cats - $22 set

Left: Lion, Japan, 4 3/4" h - $22
Right: Deer, 4 3/4" h - $20

Miscellaneous Animals

Left: Husband Kelvin, 1960, Japan, 6" h - $34
Right: Playboy Kelvin, 1960, Japan, 6" h - $34

Old Gray Mule, 5" h - $42

Duckie, Japan,
3 3/4" h - $22

Smart Cat, 6 1/8" h - $35

Left: Siamese Cats, 5" h - $58
Right: Snow Owl, Avon, 4 1/2" h - $35

Miscellaneous Animals

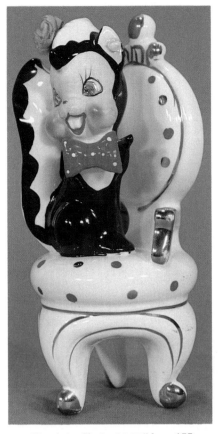

Skunk in Chair, 6 9/10" h - $55

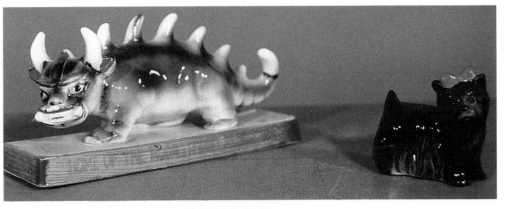

Left: Dragon, Japan, 3" h - $35
Right: Dog, 2" h - $18

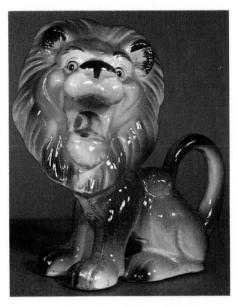

Circus Lion, 5" h - $28

Dog Decanter, 6 1/4" h
$38

Bear, 4 1/2" h - $48

Bee Sugar Shakers,
6 1/2" h - $44

Miscellaneous Monsters

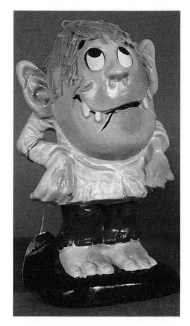

Ax Figures - $66 each
Left: 4" H   Right: 3 1/2" h

Vampire Boy, by Vampcoware,
5 1/2" h - $49

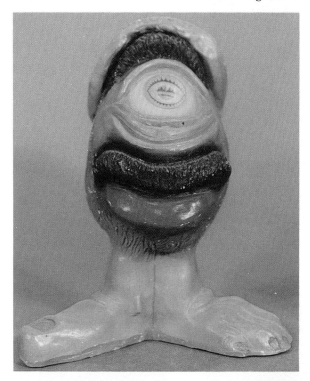

Ding Bat with flasher eye, 6 3/5" h - $149

Left: John Figure, 4 1/2" h - $88
Right: Head of Engineering, 4" h - $75

Left: Movie Star Figure,
        3" h - $86
Right: Eye to Eye Figure,
        3" h - $84

Miscellaneous Monsters

Left: Get Serious Figure, 4" h - $86
Right: You're Different, Figure, 3 1/2" h - $86

Left: Bloody Mary, 4" h - $88
Right: Best Friend, 4" h - $72

Left: Cyclops Purple People Eater Bank, Japan, 5 1/4" h - $94
Right: Brains Think Big, Japan, 5 3/8" h - $34

Left: Split Personality, 4" h - $74
Right: Headache Figure, Japan, 4" h - $69

Left: Conehead, 3 1/2" h - $58
Right: Horror Movie, 4" h - $68

Men are Beasts, 4 1/2" H - $58

Mugs

Left: Flicker Eye Mug - $18
Right: Party Character Glasses, Enesco

Party Character Glasses,
Enesco, Japan, 4 3/4" h - $18

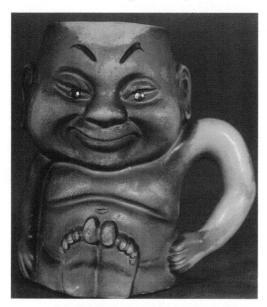

Baby Mug, 4 1/2" h - $22

Party Character Mugs, Enesco, Japan, 4 3/4" h - $18

Face Mug, 1980, Enesco - $18

Cigar Smoker Mug
$110

Party Character Glass,
Enesco, Japan, 4 3/4" h - $18

Mugs

Left: Mug, Japan, 4 7/8" h - $40
Right: Mug, Japan, 5" h - $40

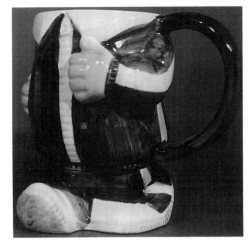

Jogging Mug, 5 1/8" h,
1978, Enesco - $20

Left: Pickled Pete Muggsy by Pfaltzgraff Pottery, Jessop - $44
Right: Cockeyed Charlie Muggsy by Pfaltzgraff Pottery, Jessop - $44

Dragon Monster Mug - $146

Left: Karol, Ted and Alice Man Mug, 1976, 3 1/4" h - $18
Right: Karol, Ted and Alice Woman Mug, 1976, 3 1/4" h - $18

Mugs

Left: Handsome Herman Muggsy
by Pfaltzgraff Pottery, Jessop - $44
Right: Hillbilly - $26

Left: Lion Stein, Kentucky Straight Bourbon
Whiskey- 86 proof, 1973, Lionstone - $89
Right: Budweiser 1986 Stein, Ceramarte Brazil
Collectors Series - $32

Left: First River Steamer 1807, Miller Steamer River Stein,
Great American Achievements 1855-1989, Brazil,
Carolina Coll. 4th Series - $32
Right: Millers Nassa Astronaut 1969 Stein, 1855-1990
5th Series - $32

Left: Small Snake Mug, 1956, St. Pierre & Patterson - $30
Right: Large Snake Mug, 1956, St. Pierre & Patterson - $25

Left: Head Mug, Japan, 4 7/8" h - $40
Right: Hillbilly, Japan, 4 1/2" h - $26

Left: Stroh's Stein Heritage Series - $32
Right: Budweiser Stein, Ceramarte Brazil
Collectors Series - $32

Nodders

Left: I'm A Lover Figure, 1961, St. Pierre &
Patterson, Japan, 6" h - $84
Right: Give Up Figure, 1961,St. Pierre &
Patterson, Japan, 7" h - $84

Left: I Work Better Under Pressure Nodder, 1961,
St. Pierre & Patterson, Japan, 6 1/2" h - $84
Right: Hurry Nodder, 1961, St. Pierre & Patterson,
Japan, 7 1/4" h - $84

Left: Convience Me Nodder, 1961, St. Pierre & Patterson,
Japan, 6 1/2" h - $84
Right: Convince Me Nodder, 1961, St. Pierre & Patterson,
Japan, 6 1/2" h - $96

Left: Drunk Nodder, 5 1/2" h - $56
Right: Old Lady Nodder, 7" h - $84

Left: Drunk Nodder, Japan,
5 3/4" h - $56
Right: Not A Millionaire
Nodder, Japan, 6" h - $56

Nodders

Left: Golfer, 1961, St. Pierre & Patterson,
Japan, 5 3/4" h - $84
Right: Bowler, 1961, St. Pierre & Patterson,
Japan, 6 1/4" h - $84

Left: Lady Figure, Japan, 4 3/4" h - $42
Right: Indian Figure, Semco, Japan, 5 3/4" h - $48

Apple A Day Nodder, 1961,
St. Pierre & Patterson, Japan,
6 1/4" h - $84

Doctor Nodder, Japan, 5 1/2" h
$56

Mummy Monoter,
Hong Kong, 5 3/4" h
$76

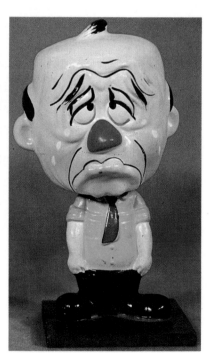

Smile Again Nodder, 1961,
St. Pierre & Patterson, Japan,
6" h - $84

Nodders

Indian Medicine Man Nodder,
6 1/2" h - $56

Will Travel Nodder, 1961,
St. Pierre & Patterson, Japan,
6 1/2" h - $84

Scottish Nodder, Japan,
6 1/2" h - $56

Knight Nodder, 1961,
St. Pierre & Patterson,
Japan, 6 1/4" h - $84

Pig Pen Nodder,
6 1/2" h - $75

Bowling Bank Nodder,
Lego, Japan, 7"h - $56

Nodders

Left: Monk, 6" h - $44
Right: Hillbilly Bank, 6 1/2" h - $46

Genius Award with Flicker Eyes,
5 1/4" h - $66

Old Man, 7 1/2" h - $56

Fisherman Caught Mermaid,
Lego, Japan, 7 1/2" h - $56

Boxer, Japan, 7 1/4" h
$56

Nodders

Brown Donkey, 6" h - $46

Deer Ceramic Nodder,
Japan, 4 1/2" h - $46

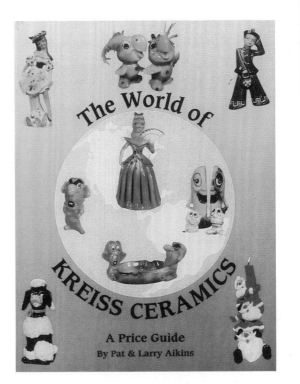

The World of
KREISS CERAMICS
A Price Guide
by
PAT & LARRY AIKINS

This book contains novelty figurines, banks, nodders, animals, salt and pepper shakers, napkin holders etc. that were made by the Kreiss Ceramic Company.

The many figures were labeled as Psycho's, Giant Psycho's, Beatnicks & Beatchicks, Elegant Heirs, Nudies, and many others.

The book is 8 1/2" x 11" with 224 pages and includes hundreds of full color photos that described and priced.

Item #1116
Only $24.95
+ $3.00 Shipping